Contents

D0306342

Spanish words are in italics, *like this*. You can find out how to say them by looking in the pronunciation guide.

Spanish around the world

People first spoke Spanish in Spain, but nowadays Spanish is the main language in 20 countries all around the world. It is also spoken by more than 45 million people in the United States.

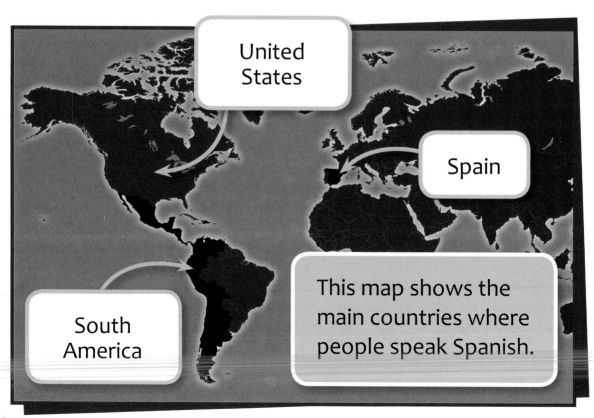

United States

Spain

South America

This map shows the main countries where people speak Spanish.

Even though English is the main language of the United States, millions of Americans speak Spanish at home.

In some Spanish-speaking countries people call Spanish *español*. In others people prefer to call Spanish *castellano*. But *español* and *castellano* are the same language.

Who speaks Spanish?

Spanish is the main language of about 350 million people around the world. Spanish is the third most spoken language in the world after Mandarin Chinese and English.

Spanish is spoken in most countries in South America.

In Spain, a *carro* is a supermarket trolley, not a car!

Spanish can sound quite different in different countries. People sometimes use different words for the same thing, too. The word for "car" is *coche* in Spain and *carro* in Mexico.

Spanish and English

Some words, like *chocolate*, are spelt the same in Spanish and English. Other words are very similar. Can you guess the meaning of the words below?

bicicleta   *fruta*   *tomate*   *familia*
(See page 32 for answers.)

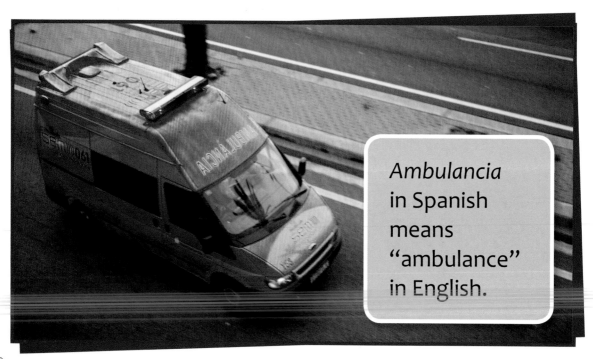

Ambulancia in Spanish means "ambulance" in English.

Bien cool! means "Really cool!" in Spanglish. *Bien* is Spanish and "cool" is English.

In the United States lots of young people speak "Spanglish". This is a mixture of English and Spanish words. It is like a new language!

Learning Spanish

Spanish uses the same alphabet as English, but it has 29 letters instead of 26. The extra letters are shown in bold below:

a b c **ch** d e f g h i j k l **ll** m n **ñ** o p q r s t u v w x y z

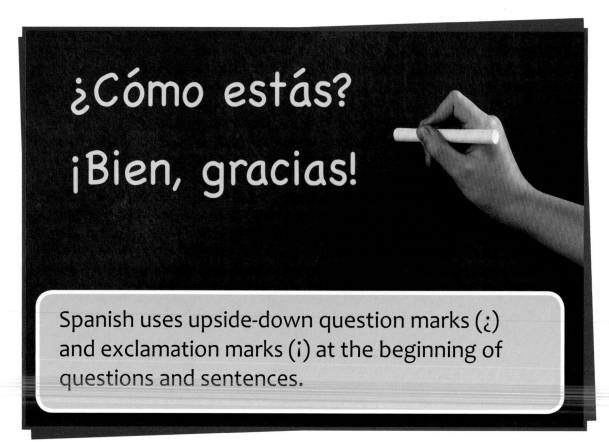

¿Cómo estás?
¡Bien, gracias!

Spanish uses upside-down question marks (¿) and exclamation marks (¡) at the beginning of questions and sentences.

The word "key" in Spanish is *llave*, but you say "ya-bay" with a "y" and a "b", not "la-vay"!

Some letters in the Spanish alphabet sound different to English. In Spain "z" is spoken like "th" in English. In South America though, "z" sounds like "s".

Saying hello and goodbye

Family and friends usually give each other a kiss on the cheek when they say hello. Men might give each other a hug or a pat on the shoulder or back.

How to say it
kiss = *beso*
hug = *abrazo*

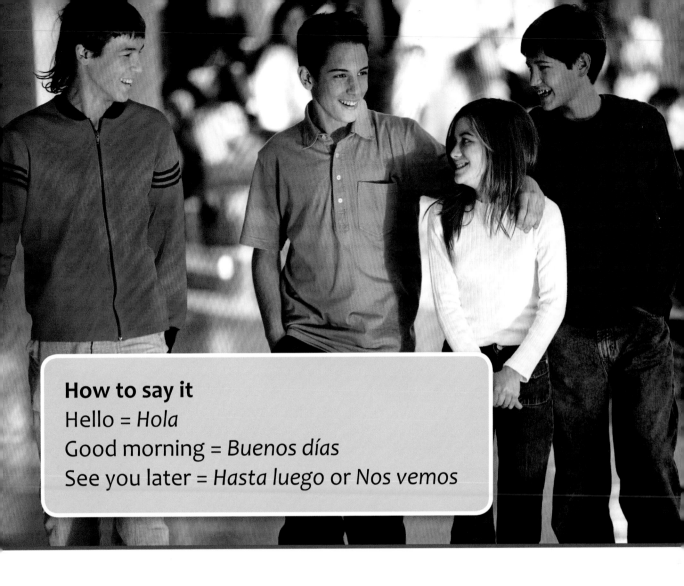

How to say it
Hello = *Hola*
Good morning = *Buenos días*
See you later = *Hasta luego* or *Nos vemos*

When people meet, they may say "*Hola*" or "*Buenos días*". "*Adiós*" means "Goodbye", but family and friends often say "*Hasta luego*" or "*Nos vemos*", too.

Talking about yourself

When people meet others for the first time they usually give their name. They may say *"Me llamo Sarah"* or *"Mi nombre es Sarah"*.

How to say it
I'm called... = *Me llamo ...*
My name is = *Mi nombre es ...*

How to say it
I'm from ... = *Soy de ...*
I live in ... = *Vivo en ...*

People often say where they are from, for example, "*Soy de España.*" ("I am from Spain.") They may say where they live, for example, "*Vivo en Valencia.*" ("I live in Valencia.")

Asking about others

It is polite to ask other people about themselves. The first thing people usually ask is someone's name. They say "*¿Cómo te llamas?*"

How to say it
What's your name? = *¿Cómo te llamas?*

How to say it
Where are you from? = *¿De dónde eres?*
Where do you live? = *¿Dónde vives?*

To ask someone where they are from people usually say "*¿De dónde eres?*" If they want to know where someone lives they say "*¿Dónde vives?*"

At home

A few people in Spain live in cave houses that are carved out of rock. Cave houses stay cool during the hot Spanish summers. They are very popular with tourists.

How to say it

house = *casa*

bedroom = *habitación*

living room = *sala*

kitchen = *cocina*

bathroom = *baño*

How to say it
hammock = *hamaca*
bed = *cama*

Some places in South America are very hot. Some people even sleep in hammocks instead of beds to stay cool. They are just as comfortable!

Family life

South American families are often larger than families in Europe. There may be lots of brothers and sisters living with their mum and dad.

How to say it
mum = *mamá*
dad = *papá*
brother = *hermano*
sister = *hermana*

How to say it
grandparent = *abuelo*
aunt = *tía*
uncle = *tío*
cousin = *primo*

Grandparents often live with the whole family. Family celebrations such as birthday parties usually include aunts, uncles, and cousins, too.

At school

Many Spanish schools start at 9 o'clock and finish at 5 o'clock. Students have a long lunch break, when they can go home, eat, and have a short nap. This nap is called a *siesta*.

How to say it
school = *escuela*
student = *estudiante*
nap = *siesta*

How to say it
class = *clase*
morning = *mañana*
afternoon = *tarde*
holidays = *vacaciones*

In Bolivia, most children have classes for four hours either in the morning or in the afternoon, from Monday to Saturday. The summer holidays are in December and January.

Sport

Football is the main sport of Spain, and there are some great players. Spain won the football World Cup in South Africa in 2010.

How to say it
sport = *deporte*
football = *fútbol*
ball = *pelota*
trophy = *trofeo*

How to say it
baseball = *béisbol*
team = *equipo*
bat = *bate*

Baseball is popular in many South American countries, such as Venezuela. Some children play in baseball teams from a very young age.

Food

People in Spanish-speaking countries eat many different foods. In Spain, people love to eat small hot or cold snacks called *tapas* or *pinchos*.

How to say it
bread = *pan*
prawns = *gambas*
ham = *jamón*
olives = *aceitunas*

How to say it
chilli = *chile*
beans = *frijoles*
meat = *carne*
cheese = *queso*

In Mexico, food made with hot chillies is popular. A *tortilla* is a flat bread, often made from corn. *Tacos* are fried *tortillas* filled with spicy beans, meat, or cheese.

27

Clothes

Many people in Spanish-speaking countries relax in casual clothes like T-shirts and jeans. Some children wear a school uniform. For work, people wear smart clothes like suits, shirts, and skirts.

How to say it
T-shirt = *camiseta*
jeans = *jeans or vaqueros*
uniform = *uniforme*

How to say it
suit = *traje*
hat = *bombín*
shawl = *chal*

In Bolivia, some women wear traditional clothes in their day-to-day lives. They often wear a bowler hat called a *bombín*. They also wear a brightly coloured shawl, and a full skirt called a *pollera*.

Pronunciation guide

English	Spanish	Pronunciation
afternoon	*tarde*	*tar-day*
aunt	*tía*	*tee-ah*
ball	*pelota*	*pay-lott-ah*
baseball	*béisbol*	*bay-is-boll*
bat	*bate*	*bah-tay*
bathroom	*baño*	*bah-nyo*
beans	*frijoles*	*free-hol-ays*
bed	*cama*	*cah-ma*
bedroom	*habitación*	*ah-bee-ta-thee-on*
bowler hat	*bombín*	*bom-bin*
bread	*pan*	*pan*
brother	*hermano*	*air-man-oh*
cheese	*queso*	*kay-so*
chilli	*chile*	*chee-lay*
class	*clase*	*clah-say*
cousin	*primo*	*pree-mo*
dad	*papá*	*pah-pah*
football	*fútbol*	*foot-boll*
good morning	*buenos días*	*boo-ay-nos dee-as*
grandparent	*abuelo*	*ah-boo-ay-lo*
ham	*jamón*	*hah-mone*
hammock	*hamaca*	*ah-mah-cah*
hello	*hola*	*oh-lah*
holidays	*vacaciones*	*bah-cah-thee-on-ess*
house	*casa*	*cah-sah*
hug	*abrazo*	*ah-brah-tho*
I live in ...	*Vivo en ...*	*Bee-boh en*

I'm called ...	Me llamo ...	May yah-mo
I'm from ...	Soy de ...	Soy day
jeans	jeans	jeens
kiss	beso	bay-so
kitchen	cocina	coh-thee-nah
living room	sala	sah-lah
meat	carne	car-nay
morning	mañana	mah-nyah-na
mum	mamá	mah-mah
My name is ...	Mi nombre es ...	Mee nom-bray ess
nap	siesta	see-ess-tah
olives	aceitunas	ah-thay-too-nass
prawns	gambas	gam-bass
school	escuela	es-coo-ay-lah
see you later	hasta luego	as-tah loo-ay-go
see you later	nos vemos	nos bay-mos
shawl	chal	chal
shirt	camisa	cah-mee-sah
sister	hermana	air-man-ah
Spain	España	Es-pa-nya
sport	deporte	day-por-tay
student/pupil	estudiante	es-too-dee-an-tay
suit	traje	trah-hay
T-shirt	camiseta	cam-ee-say-tah
team	equipo	ay-kee-po
trophy	trofeo	tro-fay-o
uncle	tío	tee-o
uniform	uniforme	oo-nee-for-may
What's your name?	¿Cómo te llamas?	Co-moh tay yah-mas
Where are you from?	¿De dónde eres?	Day don-day air-ess
Where do you live?	¿Dónde vives?	Don-day bee-bess

Find out more

Books

Collins Very First Spanish Dictionary (Collins, 2009)

My First Spanish Book: A Bilingual Introduction to Words, Numbers, Shapes and Colours, Mandy Stanley (Kingfisher, 2007)

Websites

kids.nationalgeographic.com/kids/places/find/spain/

www.bbc.co.uk/schools/primaryspanish/

Index

Meaning of the words on page 8

bicicleta = bicycle

tomate = tomato

fruta = fruit

familia = family
